BLANK SPACES

AN UNOFFICIAL TAYLOR SWIFT FAN JOURNAL

PENGUIN B

PENGUIN BOOKS

UK | USA | Canada | Ireland | Australia
India | New Zealand | South Africa | China

Penguin Random House Australia is part of the Penguin Random House group of companies whose addresses can be found at global.penguinrandomhouse.com.

First published by Penguin Books, an imprint of Penguin Random House Australia Pty Ltd, in 2024

Cover illustration by Melissa Lane
Cover and internal design by Caroline Lee © Penguin Random House Australia Pty Ltd

Internal images: © 2023 Eras Tour – Kansas City Night Two: Fernando Leon/TAS23/Getty Images Entertainment via Getty Images; Taylor Swift Visit MTV's 'TRL': Gary Gershoff/WireImage via Getty Images; 2023 Eras Tour – Cincinnati: Taylor Hill/TAS23/Getty Images Entertainment via Getty Images; 2018 Reputation Stadium Tour: Kevin Winter/Getty Images Entertainment via Getty Images; 2022 US Entertainment Music Award MTV Show: ANGELA WEISS/AFP via Getty Images; 2009 CMT Music Awards: Kevin Mazur/WireImage via Getty Images; 1989 World Tour with Selena Gomez: Christopher Polk/TAS/Getty Images Entertainment via Getty Images; 2011 Speak Now World Tour: Larry Busacca/Getty Images Entertainment via Getty Images; 2013 RED Tour – Newark: Kevin Mazur/TAS/Getty Images Entertainment via Getty Images; 2023 Eras Tour – Kansas City Night One: John Shearer/TAS23/Getty Images Entertainment via Getty Images.

Printed and bound in China

A catalogue record for this book is available from the National Library of Australia

ISBN 978 1 76134 710 8 (Paperback)

Penguin Random House Australia uses papers that are natural and recyclable products, made from wood grown in sustainable forests. The logging and manufacture processes are expected to conform to the environmental regulations of the country of origin.

penguin.com.au

We at Penguin Random House Australia acknowledge that Aboriginal and Torres Strait Islander peoples are the Traditional Custodians and the first storytellers of the lands on which we live and work. We honour Aboriginal and Torres Strait Islander peoples' continuous connection to Country, waters, skies and communities. We celebrate Aboriginal and Torres Strait Islander stories, traditions and living cultures; and we pay our respects to Elders past and present.

WARNING!

If you are OBSESSED with Taylor Swift . . .
this book could worsen your condition.

If you already *THINK* about, *READ* about and *MENTION* Taylor Swift in everyday conversation, now is the time to **SERIOUSLY** consider if you should go any further.

Benefits

- This journal will not judge you.
- Your hater friends and family will enjoy the break.
- There will be lessons learned in the pages turned.

Dear Reader,

Maybe you're thinking, why would you create a journal inspired by the music of Taylor Swift? Or, if you've bought this, maybe you're not thinking that.

But, here it is . . .

Taylor Swift has written a song for every situation in your life. One of the main reasons she has achieved such huge popularity is the diverse range of interpersonal relationships she covers in her music. The lyrics are both specific and yet entirely relatable.

We know that Taylor draws from her own emotions to write her lyrics, and we, in turn, experience our own emotions from listening to her songs.

So what better way to process those emotions than by reflecting on your life and experiences the same way Taylor does? Now is your chance.

Maybe reduce your stress.
Definitely have fun.

. . . ***Ready For It?***

INSTRUCTIONS

Grab a fountain pen, a **GLITTER** gel pen, or if you're really committed . . . a quill.

You'll be writing, drawing and **PASTING IN** your favourite pictures. Be ready with pencils, pens, glitter, glue and sticky tape. Plus, whatever other decorations you can think of to **BEJEWEL** your book!

THERE ARE NO RULES.

Be as *messy* or neat as you want.

Don't like a prompt? Ignore it! Put something else in.

Can't answer a question now? Come back to it later.

Got too much to say? Paste in some extra paper and fold it over.

This is the story of **YOU**.

NOSTALGIA

Distraction

OBSESSION

Love

Friendship

Introspection

HEARTBREAK

Escapism

'PEOPLE HAVEN'T ALWAYS BEEN THERE FOR ME, BUT MUSIC ALWAYS HAS.'
TAYLOR SWIFT, TWITTER, 8 OCTOBER 2013

IT'S ME, HI!

This book belongs to:

____

YOUR BIRTHDAY:

YOUR STAR SIGN:

YOUR FAVOURITE NUMBER:

YOUR FAVOURITE COLOUR:

YOUR PETS' NAME/S:

TAYLOR'S BIRTHDAY:

____

TAYLOR'S STAR SIGN:

____

TAYLOR'S FAVOURITE NUMBER:

____

TAYLOR'S FAVOURITE COLOUR:

____

TAYLOR'S PETS' NAME/S:

____

FAN BIO

TOP FIVE SONGS

1. ______

2. ______

3. ______

4. ______

5. ______

FAVOURITE ALBUM

FAVOURITE COLLABORATION

FAVOURITE ALBUM COVER

FAVOURITE MUSIC VIDEO

Nostalgia

Hold on to the memories.

Your memories are unique to you. The more you think about them, the less likely you are to forget. Journal them here for safekeeping.

Nice to meet you.

What is your first Taylor Swift memory?

WRITE A LETTER TO YOUR
FIFTEEN-YEAR-OLD SELF.

Most iconic Taylor Swift moments . . .

WHAT MAKES YOU WISH YOU'D NEVER GROWN UP?

CAPTURE
EVERY
MOMENT.

Photos or printouts on
these pages of you and
your friends!

A picture that you wish you could burn!

HAVE YOU SEEN TAYLOR SWIFT ON TOUR?

May these memories break your fall:

YOUR FAVOURITE

PICTURES OF TAYLOR.

CUSTOMISE YOUR OWN CONCERT TICKET

SURPRISE SONGS

YOUR FAVOURITE ERAS TOUR MOMENT

YOUR ERAS TOUR OUTFIT

WHAT ARE SOME MOMENTS WHEN TAYLOR HAS BEEN **THE MAN**?

WHEN IN YOUR LIFE HAVE YOU BEEN

THE MAN?

When did you have the time of your life and who with?

Today was a **FAIRYTALE.**

Plan the perfect day.

THE OLD YOU VS

THE NEW YOU

Distraction

You have things to do.
We all have things to do.

But sometimes . . . you don't *WANT* to do the things you have to do!

Luckily, you *NEED* to do all of these activities to complete your journal. It's important to finish the things you've started.

DRAW AS MANY THIRTEENS AS YOU CAN TO FILL THIS PAGE –

GET CREATIVE!

On your way home, write a poem.

draw hearts in the byline

Design the perfect DRESS.

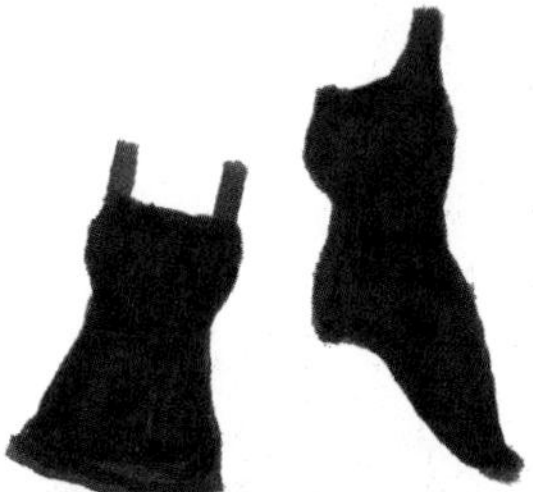

Create your own LABYRINTH.

COLOUR IN:

BLANK SPACE

Uncharted territory . . .

Design the aesthetic of a new era!

Test your instant recall - name the song from just two words.

1) Space. What?

2) Pinned-up hair

3) Cold hard

4) Rodeo clowns

5) Worn-out jeans

6) Tea time

7) I'm paralysed

8) Ten months

9) Tangled up

10) Red, underlined

11) American smile

Are you a mastermind?

GUESS THESE CONNECTIONS TO TAYLOR SWIFT!

PRINCE HARRY

R_______

CLUE: HAS A DOLLAR SIGN IN THEIR NAME

A___ R____

CLUE: IS A MODEL

K_______
J______

G___
H____

TAYLOR SWIFT

PRINCE HARRY — RIHANNA — A$AP ROCKY — KENDALL JENNER — GIGI HADID — TAYLOR SWIFT

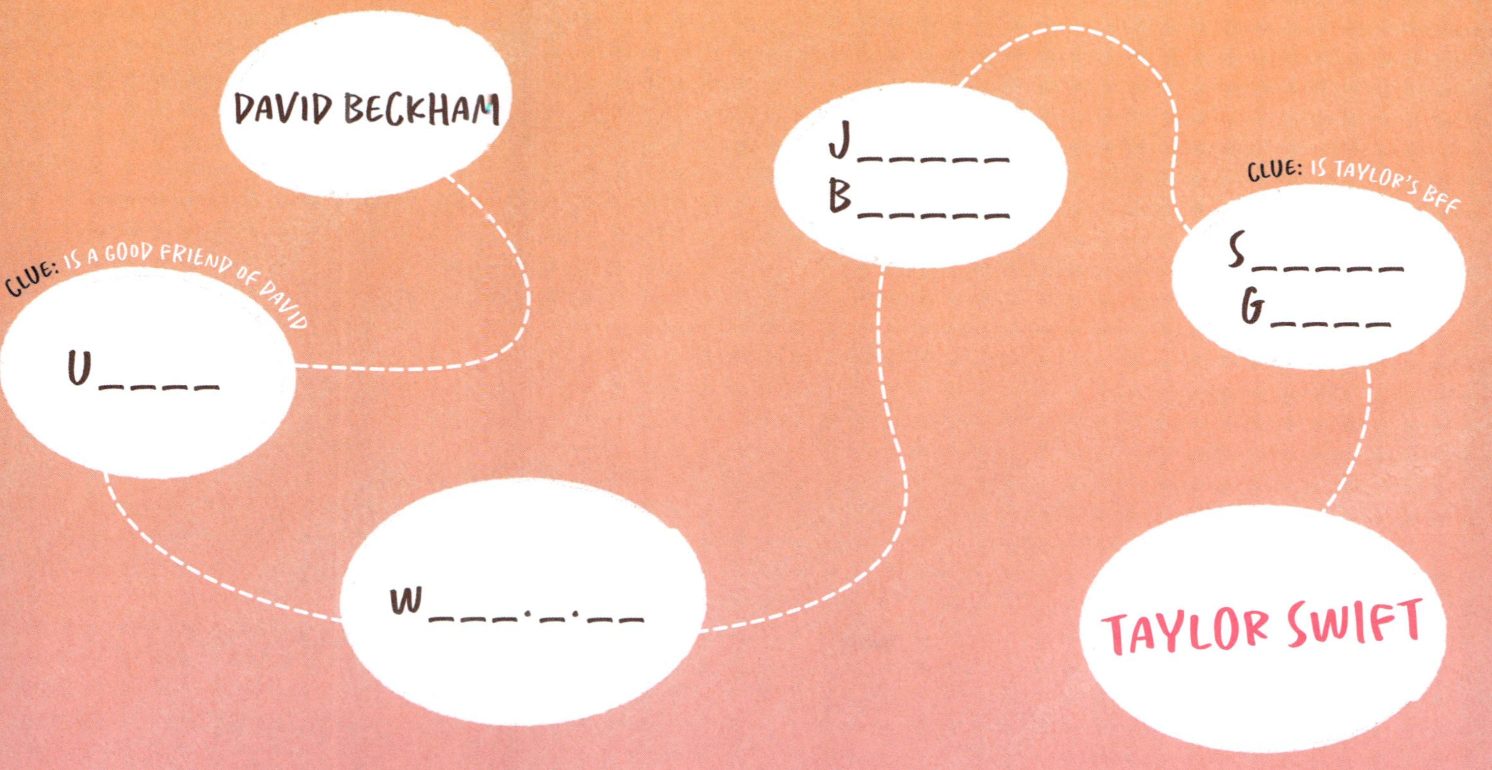

DAVID BECKHAM – USHER – WILL.I.AM – JUSTIN BIEBER – SELENA GOMEZ – TAYLOR SWIFT

MALALA YOUSAFZAI

P_______
C_____

A___
H_______

CLUE: STARRED IN THE DARK NIGHT TRILOGY

C________
B___

CLUE: STARRED IN THE DARK NIGHT TRILOGY

J_______
L_______

TAYLOR SWIFT

MALALA YOUSAFZAI – PRIYANKA CHOPRA – ANNE HATHAWAY – CHRISTIAN BALE – JENNIFER LAWRENCE – TAYLOR SWIFT

SIR DAVID ATTENBOROUGH

J_ _ _ _ _ _ _
C_ _ _ _ _ _ _ _

O_ _ _ _
I_ _ _ _

CLUE: STARRED IN DUNE

T_ _ _ _ _ _ _ _
C_ _ _ _ _ _ _ _

CLUE: STARRED IN DUNE

Z_ _ _ _ _ _

TAYLOR SWIFT

SIR DAVID ATTENBOROUGH – JESSICA CHASTAIN – OSCAR ISAAC – TIMOTHÉE CHALAMET – ZENDAYA – TAYLOR SWIFT

SONG BATTLE I

Shake It Off

22

Getaway Car

Cornelia Street

Enchanted

All Too Well

Cruel Summer

New Romantics

SONG BATTLE II

Tim McGraw

White Horse

The Alchemy

Paper Rings

I Knew You Were Trouble

I Did Something Bad

August

Maroon

SOMETIMES THINGS AREN'T QUITE HOW YOU IMAGINED THEM.

WHICH LYRIC WOULD YOU CHANGE, AND TO WHAT?

STARBUCKS LOVERS

Write misheard lyrics here.

NOWHERE

U F K W R K T Y Y E A Y X M V Q T T S I
K B P F F B K Q G M I D N I G H T S D T
A O S L E W E J R O I N U J N G X V E G
O M Y I H G H P U Z H D T O T C J G N L
L X E X B Y D Y I T O L U R E R K F C T
B U P R W B B X I J U S H D G A R I H I
U X S G I Q S D N A P P Y Z O U O O A B
S E V E N C E A V X P K M T E T Y Y N L
K D H M S R A E G K M A E R S U W S T E
C H J I E N W N E I R V O T D M E P E A
A B K M O X A S A J T L R E C N N A D C
R E U N Z A I K O M K T R M R L R R X H
D J P E X Q T R E L H Z A N H J R K Z E
I E W N J W I C O A F E A R L E S S N L
G W A D Q E Y F H N E W B L I Q H F C L
A E R G V I O D E I T F I W S U U L X A
N L G A V X A H M P Y O Y S F U S Y R H
T E C M E S T N E E T R I H T D T J J D
R D M E P S T Y L E Y S G P B E Q E N D
S U M W K V V R T W B T Q N P V W L L T

TO HIDE

MEREDITH	SNAKE	JUNIOR JEWELS
THIRTEEN	END GAME	FEARLESS
FOLKLORE	MIDNIGHTS	RED
SWIFTIE	ENCHANTED	BEJEWELED
BLEACHELLA	VAULT	SEVEN
SAGITTARIUS	NEW YORK	MARJORIE
AUTUMN	STYLE	MCGRAW
SPARKS FLY	CARDIGAN	AMERICANA

Tay to Z!

No, actually this is A-Z.
The complete list of Taylor Swift songs sorted in alphabetical order.
Protect your reputation by getting them all.

NB: Titles beginning with 'The' are under the first letter of the second word.

These are songs written AND performed by Taylor Swift as of May 2024. It does not include covers or songs where she is featured. Remixes are not included either, so each song is only listed once.

*Well, except one 10 minute song that can't go unmentioned – there is always an exception to the rules.

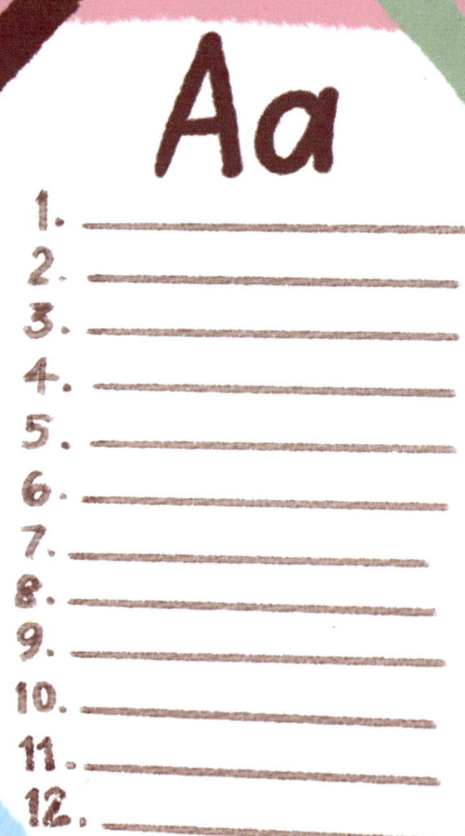

Bb

1. ______
2. ______
3. ______
4. ______
5. ______
6. ______
7. ______
8. ______
9. ______
10. ______
11. ______
12. ______
13. ______
14. ______
15. ______
16. ______
17. ______

# #

1. ______
2. ______

Cc

1.
2.
3.
4.
5.
6.
7.
8.
9.
10.
11.
12.
13.
14.
15.
16.
17.
18.
19.
20.
21.
22.

Dd

1.
2.
3.
4.
5.
6.
7.
8.
9.
10.
11.

Ee

1.
2.
3.
4.
5.
6.
7.
8.

Ff

1. ______
2. ______
3. ______
4. ______
5. ______
6. ______
7. ______
8. ______
9. ______

Gg

1. ______
2. ______
3. ______
4. ______
5. ______
6. ______
7. ______

Hh

1. ______________________
2. ______________________
3. ______________________
4. ______________________
5. ______________________
6. ______________________
7. ______________________
8. ______________________
9. ______________________

Ii

1. __________
2. __________
3. __________
4. __________
5. __________
6. __________
7. __________
8. __________
9. __________
10. __________
11. __________
12. __________
13. __________
14. __________
15. __________
16. __________
17. __________
18. __________
19. __________
20. __________
21. __________
22. __________

23. ____________________

24. ____________________

25. ____________________

1. ____________________

Kk

1. ____________________

2. ____________________

LI

1. ____________________
2. ____________________
3. ____________________
4. ____________________
5. ____________________
6. ____________________
7. ____________________
8. ____________________
9. ____________________
10. ____________________
11. ____________________
12. ____________________
13. ____________________
14. ____________________

Mm

1. ______
2. ______
3. ______
4. ______
5. ______
6. ______
7. ______
8. ______
9. ______
10. ______
11. ______
12. ______
13. ______
14. ______
15. ______
16. ______
17. ______
18. ______

Nn

1.
2.
3.
4.
5.
6.

Qq 1. ______

Rr

1. ______
2. ______
3. ______
4. ______
5. ______
6. ______

Ss

1. ____________
2. ____________
3. ____________
4. ____________
5. ____________
6. ____________
7. ____________
8. ____________
9. ____________
10. ____________
11. ____________
12. ____________
13. ____________
14. ____________
15. ____________
16. ____________
17. ____________
18. ____________
19. ____________
20. ____________
21. ____________
22. ____________
23. ____________
24. ____________
25. ____________

Tt

1.
2.
3.
4.
5.
6.
7.
8.
9.
10.
11.
12.
13.
14.
15.
16.

Uu

1.

Vv

1. ______________

2. ______________

Ww

1. ______________
2. ______________
3. ______________
4. ______________
5. ______________
6. ______________
7. ______________
8. ______________
9. ______________
10. ______________
11. ______________

X

marks the spot, but not the first letter of a Taylor Swift song. Maybe one day!

Zz.

Obsession

Your friends and family are SICK TO DEATH of hearing about Taylor Swift!

That's okay, indulge your obsession by overthinking and overanalysing every single song and album ranking. Some things are best kept in your journal anyway.

'THE WORST KIND OF PERSON IS SOMEONE WHO MAKES SOMEONE FEEL BAD, DUMB OR STUPID FOR BEING EXCITED ABOUT SOMETHING.'

Taylor Swift, Live Lounge interview with Clara Amfo on BBC Radio 1, 13 September 2019

CAN'T BELIEVE WE MIGHT NEVER HAVE HEARD THESE!

Your favourite vault tracks?

RANK YOUR FAVOURITE

2

3

4

5

6

ERAS 1 TO 11

7

8

9

10

11

AND EXPLAIN WHY.

THE FIRST SONG THAT COMES TO MIND WHEN YOU HEAR THE WORD . . .

DRUNK

2am

RAIN

forget

Baby

TIME

Love

THEY'RE GONNA BE TIMELESS

NO ONE CAN ARGUE WITH YOU ON THESE TOP FIVE MOST POPULAR SONGS.

LET'S GO! It's time to **BATTLE** out the case for some underrated bops, too.

'I've seen her change the music industry first-hand . . . She's amazing for being a champion, and making things better for the generations to come. She has a long history of rightly exposing some real darkness in the music industry. And I'm personally thankful for it, outside of our friendship and working relationship, just as an artist.'

JACK ANTONOFF, *NME*, 30 JULY 2021

SONG BATTLE III

Love Story

You Belong With Me

The Man

Mad Woman

Anti-Hero

Guilty as Sin?

right where you left me

the lakes

REMEMBER THAT . . .

absolutely banging outfit Taylor wore that time. What was that one?

time Taylor said that amazing thing. Write it here as an affirmation:

WHAT SONGS DO YOU SING

IN THE SHOWER?

DRIVING YOUR CAR?

WALKING?

CLEANING?

RANK EVERY SONG ON

Taylor Swift

Taylor Swift scrapbook

RANK EVERY SONG ON

Fearless
(Taylor's Version)

Fearless scrapbook

RANK EVERY SONG ON

Speak Now
(Taylor's Version)

Speak Now scrapbook

RANK EVERY SONG ON

Red (Taylor's Version)

Red scrapbook

RANK EVERY SONG ON

1989 (Taylor's Version)

1989 scrapbook

RANK EVERY SONG ON

reputation

reputation scrapbook

RANK EVERY SONG ON

Lover

Lover scrapbook

RANK EVERY SONG ON

folklore

folklore scrapbook

RANK EVERY SONG ON

evermore

evermore scrapbook

RANK EVERY SONG ON

Midnights

Midnights scrapbook

RANK EVERY SONG ON

THE TORTURED POETS DEPARTMENT

THE TORTURED POETS DEPARTMENT
scrapbook

Love

Taylor has spent her whole life trying to put it into words.

Your turn to try.

DECORATE YOUR OWN HOUSE.

If all you could do is put a message in a bottle, who would it be for and what would it say?

Lyrics that describe

your current situation.

Are you a hopeless romantic?

Plan out your dream date.

WHAT ARE THE BEST *sweet nothings?*

What is Taylor's best advice for how a man should apologise to a woman?

What is yours?

YOU ARE IN LOVE.

THIS IS HOW YOU KNOW:

It's your big day!

Wedding waltz options:

LOVING THEM IS LIKE . . .

Friendship

FRIENDSHIP IS JUST AS IMPORTANT AS ROMANTIC LOVE. FORGET THE 'BAD BLOOD' AND FOCUS ON THE 'MAD LOVE'.

HERE'S A TOAST TO YOUR REAL FRIENDS!

Assemble your

own squad.

WHAT LYRICS MAKE YOU THINK OF YOUR FRIENDS?

IT'S NICE TO HAVE A FRIEND.

This page is to rave about your bff.

MAKE THE FRIENDSHIP BRACELETS.

USE THIS PAGE TO PLAN YOUR FRIENDSHIP BRACELETS

OR SHARE PHOTOS OF THE ONES YOU'VE MADE!

Karma is a cat.

Share a photo or drawing of your furry friend.

NEVER GO OUT OF STYLE:

DECORATE YOUR OWN SHIRT.

WHO WOULD YOU WANT NEXT TO YOU IN A GETAWAY CAR?

AND WHERE WOULD YOUR IDEAL DESTINATION BE?

LONG STORY SHORT.

Tell a story that fits this page.

BEHIND EVERY TAYLOR SWIFT FAN IS SOMEONE BECOMING ONE.
EXPLAIN YOUR FAN STORY.

THE MOST STRUCTURALLY

SOUND BRIDGE OF ALL TIME

Best believe you're still BEJEWELED.

Cover this page in glitter.

Heartbreak

There's a Taylor Swift song for every situation. No matter what has happened, who has let you down, how you feel . . . Taylor's got you covered.

'Your feelings are so important to write down, to capture and to remember because today you're heartbroken, but tomorrow you'll be in love again.'

TAYLOR SWIFT, *SEVENTEEN* MAGAZINE, 20 JANUARY 2009

LYRICS THAT MAKE YOU WANT TO CRY.

WE ARE NEVER EVER GETTING BACK TOGETHER

____

[insert name here]

I KNEW YOU WERE TROUBLE WHEN . . .

NOTHING LIKE A MAD WOMAN.

Who made you like that?
Get it all out of your system here.

A moment you knew it was

TIME TO GO.

But I've got me.

THINGS YOU LOVE ABOUT YOURSELF THAT NO ONE CAN TAKE AWAY!

WHAT MAKES YOU MAD

OR PUSHES YOUR BUTTONS?

MOST UNHINGED TAYLOR LYRICS:

DRAW THE WHOLE SKY.

LYRICS TO WORK

THROUGH ANGER

SOUNDTRACKS FOR EVERY SEASON.

SPRING

SUMMER

PICK AN ALBUM FOR EACH.

AUTUMN

WINTER

Introspection

SOMETIMES THE PROBLEM IS . . .
YOU?

STARE DIRECTLY INTO
THE MIRROR.

FOOLISH ONE, we all make errors. Some of them we can laugh off. Others we might still be thinking about.

Write down some of yours and purge
them from your mind . . .

DON'T WASTE TIME.

ONLY THE YOUNG CAN . . .

I want to be defined by . . .

Who or what is your guiding light?

Be

FEARLESS.

Your

bravest

moments . . .

IT'S TIME TO WRECK YOUR PLANS.

Sometimes what you thought would be isn't meant to be.

What have you left behind or what should you?

WHAT ADVICE WOULD YOU GIVE TO YOUR **22**-YEAR-OLD SELF?

IF THIS WAS A MOVIE,

what would your happy ending be?

What is your

Wildest

Dream?

An EPIPHANY you had.

SNOW ON THE BEACH is weird. What natural phenomena have you seen? Draw or describe them.

Would've, Could've, Should've . . .

DO YOU HAVE ANY REGRETS?

Create your own mood board

for a holiday house.

'Taylor reminds me of myself in her determination and her childlike nature. It's an innocence that's so special and so rare. This girl writes the songs that make the whole world sing, like Neil Diamond or Elton John. She sings, she writes, she performs, she plays great guitar.

'. . . It's women like her who are going to save the music business.'

STEVIE NICKS, *TIME* MAGAZINE, 29 APRIL 2010

TAYLOR HAS MAIN CHARACTER ENERGY.

WHAT CAN YOU LEARN FROM HER THAT YOU COULD TRY?

YOU NEED TO

THINGS YOU DO TO WIND DOWN AND

CALM DOWN

DE-STRESS FROM THE DAY

Colours mentioned in Taylor's songs and what they represent to you.

WHAT KEEPS YOU UP AT NIGHT?

USE THIS SPACE TO WRITE DOWN YOUR MIDNIGHT MUSINGS, MEMORIES OR MISTAKES.

DESCRIBE YOURSELF USING **13** TAYLOR SWIFT LYRICS THAT COME TO MIND.

Escapism

Can you feel this magic in the air?

Storytelling has a transformative power.
Write your own folklore.

Note down SEVEN memories you cherish.

I KNOW PLACES.

Every place/city/street/country Taylor has mentioned in her music.

Take me to the ______

Where/what is your happy place? Describe it.

When did you have a hard time adjusting?

MOVIES AND BOOKS THAT

TAYLOR SWIFT

FEARLESS

SPEAK NOW

RED

1989

REPUTATION

REMIND YOU OF EACH ERA

LOVER

FOLKLORE

EVERMORE

MIDNIGHTS

TTPD

Dear Taylor . . .

WRITE YOUR OWN LETTER TO TAYLOR SWIFT.

IT'S A LOVE STORY.

Our enthusiastic team of creators includes Belinda Conners, Vishali Seshadri, Caroline Lee, Shané Oosthuizen, Jess De Caria, Lydia Burgham and Mel Lane. And we extend our special thanks to David Chin.

BLANK SPACES was written, illustrated and designed BY Taylor Swift Fans FOR Taylor Swift Fans.

We believe it is an acknowledgement of the influence Taylor Swift has on popular culture, on artistry and even on our personal lives. She is one of the biggest stars on the planet and yet when she describes her emotions, she is describing exactly the same feelings as we experience.

We are so lucky to have a soundtrack for all situations in our lives and we look forward to hearing more. Of course, we never know what Taylor might do next! reputation TV? Debut TV? TS12? Like you, we will be there for all of it.

Hopefully you have had fun writing in and decorating this journal, revelling in the genius that is Taylor, and the uniqueness that is YOU.